My Little Psalms

**Illustrations by
Stephanie McFetridge Britt**

Compiled by Brenda C. Ward

WORD PUBLISHING
Dallas•London•Vancouver•Melbourne

My Little Psalms

In order to simplify text for children, some partial verses have been used.

MANAGING EDITOR: Laura Minchew
PROJECT EDITOR: Beverly Phillips

Library of Congress Cataloging-in-Publication Data:

My little psalms / illustrated by Stephanie McFetridge Britt; compiled by Brenda C. Ward.

p. cm.

Summary: An illustrated collection of verses from thirty-one psalms taken from the International Children's Bible, New Century Version.

ISBN 0-8499-1193-1

1. Bible. O.T. Psalms—Paraphrases, English. [1. Bible O.T. Psalms—Paraphrases.] I. Britt, Stephanie, ill. II. Ward, Brenda.

BS1440.W35W37   1995

223'.205208–dc20

95–1446
CIP
AC

Printed in the United States of America

95 96 97 98 99 00 LBM 9 8 7 6 5 4 3 2 1

CONTENTS

God Is Great . . .   10

Psalm 33:5–8   Psalm 93:3–4
Psalm 104:1–3   Psalm 40:5
Psalm 19:1–4   Psalm 46:10

God Is Good . . .   24

Psalm 23:1–3   Psalm 119:137–138
Psalm 36:6–7   Psalm 33:13–15
Psalm 145:13–16   Psalm 78:1–4

Let Us Thank Him . . .   38

Psalm 118:28–29   Psalm 52:8–9
Psalm 100:4–5   Psalm 92:4–5
Psalm 47:1–2   Psalm 105:1–3

Let Us Praise Him . . .   52

Psalm 63:3–5   Psalm 148:1–5
Psalm 89:15–16   Psalm 113:3–4
Psalm 104:33–34   Psalm 30:4–5

Let Us Follow Him . . .   66

Psalm 34:11–14   Psalm 19:7–9
Psalm 16:7–8   Psalm 1:1–2
Psalm 37:23–24   Psalm 25:4–5

Let Us Love Him, As We Should.   80

Psalm 71:5–6   Psalm 91:14–16
Psalm 116:1–2   Psalm 139:13–14
Psalm 63:1–3   Psalm 89:1–2
Psalm 63:6–8

GOD is GREAT

The Lord's love fills the earth.

The sky was made at the Lord's command.

By the breath from his mouth, he made all the stars.

He gathered the water in the sea into a heap.

He made the great ocean stay in its place.

All the earth should worship the Lord.

The whole world should fear him.

—PSALM 33:5–8

My whole being, praise the Lord.

Lord my God, you are very great.

You are clothed with glory and majesty.

You wear light like a robe.

You stretch out the skies like a tent.

You build your room above the clouds.

You make the clouds your chariot.

You ride on the wings of the wind.

—PSALM 104:1–3

The heavens tell the glory of God.

And the skies announce what his hands have made.

Day after day they tell the story.

Night after night they tell it again.

They have no speech or words.

They don't make any sound to be heard.

But their message goes out through all the world.

It goes everywhere on earth.

—PSALM 19:1–4

Lord, the seas rise up.
The seas raise their voice.
The seas lift up their pounding waves.
The sound of the water is loud.
The ocean waves are powerful.
But the Lord above is much greater.

—PSALM 93:3–4

Lord our God, you have
done many miracles.
Your plans for us are many.
If I tried to tell them all,
there would be too many to
count.

—Psalm 40:5

God says, "Be quiet and know that I am God.

I will be supreme over all the nations.

I will be supreme in the earth."

—Psalm 46:10

GOD iS GOOD

The Lord is my shepherd.
I have everything I need.
He gives me rest in green
pastures.
He leads me to calm water.
He gives me new strength.
For the good of his name,
he leads me on paths that are
right.

—PSALM 23:1–3

Lord, you protect both men and animals.

God, your love is so precious!

You protect people as a bird protects her young under her wings.

—PSALM 36:6–7

The Lord will keep his promises.

With love he takes care of all he has made.

The Lord helps those who have been defeated.

He takes care of those who are in trouble.

All living things look to you for food.

And you give it to them at the right time.

You open your hand, and you satisfy all living things.

—PSALM 145:13–16

Lord, you do what is right.
And your laws are fair.
The rules you commanded are
right and completely trustworthy.

—PSALM 119:137–138

The Lord looks down
from heaven.

He sees every person.

From his throne he watches
everyone who lives on earth.

He made their hearts.

He understands everything
they do.

—PSALM 33:13–15

My people, listen to my teaching.

Listen to what I say.

I will speak using stories.

I will tell things that have been secret since long ago.

We have heard them and know them.

Our fathers told them to us.

We will not keep them from our children.

We will tell those who come later about the praises of the Lord.

We will tell about his power and the miracles he has done.

—Psalm 78:1–4

LET US THANK HIM

You are my God, and I
will thank you.

You are my God, and I will
praise your greatness.

Thank the Lord because he is
good.

His love continues forever.

—PSALM 118:28–29

Come into his city with songs of thanksgiving.

Come into his courtyards with songs of praise.

Thank him, and praise his name.

The Lord is good. His love continues forever.

His loyalty continues from now on.

—PSALM 100:4–5

Clap your hands, all you
people.

Shout to God with joy.

The Lord Most High is
wonderful.

He is the great King over all the
earth!

—PSALM 47:1–2

I trust God's love forever and ever.

God, I will thank you forever for what you have done.

With those who worship you, I will trust you because you are good.

—PSALM 52:8–9

Lord, you have made
me happy by what you
have done.

I will sing for joy about what
your hands have done.

Lord, you have done such
great things!

How deep are your thoughts!

—PSALM 92:4–5

Give thanks to the Lord
and pray to him.
Tell the nations what he has
done.
Sing to him. Sing praises to him.
Tell about all the wonderful
things he has done.
Be glad that you are his.

—PSALM 105:1–3

LET US PRAISE
HIM

I will praise you.

I will praise you as long as I live.

I will lift up my hands in prayer to your name.

I will be content as if I had eaten the best foods.

My lips will sing. My mouth will praise you.

—Psalm 63:3–5

Happy are the people who know how to praise you.

Lord, let them live in the light of your presence.

In your name they rejoice all the time.

They praise your goodness.

—Psalm 89:15–16

I will sing to the Lord all
  my life.

I will sing praises to my God as
  long as I live.

May my thoughts please him.

I am happy in the Lord.

—Psalm 104:33–34

Praise the Lord!

Praise the Lord from the heavens.

Praise him high above the earth.

Praise him, all you angels.

Praise him, all you armies of heaven.

Praise him, sun and moon.

Praise him, all you shining stars.

Praise him, highest heavens and you waters above the sky.

Let them praise the Lord because they were created by his command.

—PSALM 148:1–5

The Lord's name should be praised
from where the sun rises to where it sets.
The Lord is supreme over all the nations.
His glory reaches to the skies.

—Psalm 113:3–4

Sing praises to the Lord,
you who belong to him.

Praise his holy name.

His anger lasts only a moment.

But his kindness lasts for a
lifetime.

Crying may last for a night.

But joy comes in the morning.

—PSALM 30:4–5

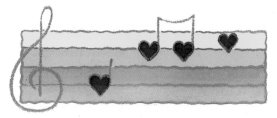

LET US FOLLOW
HiM

Children, come and listen
to me.

I will teach you to worship the
Lord.

You must do these things
to enjoy life and have many
happy days.

You must not say evil things.

You must not tell lies.

Stop doing evil and do good.

Look for peace and work for it.

—Psalm 34:11–14

I praise the Lord because he guides me.

Even at night, I feel his leading.

I keep the Lord before me always.

Because he is close by my side I will not be hurt.

—Psalm 16:7–8

When a man's steps follow the Lord,

God is pleased with his ways.

If he stumbles, he will not fall, because the Lord holds his hand.

—PSALM 37:23–24

The Lord's teachings are
  perfect.
They give new strength.
The Lord's rules can be trusted.
They make plain people wise.
The Lord's orders are right.
They make people happy.
The Lord's commands are pure.
They light up the way.
It is good to respect the Lord.
That respect will last forever.

—PSALM 19:7–9

Happy is the person who
doesn't listen to the wicked.

He doesn't go where sinners go.

He doesn't do what bad
people do.

He loves the Lord's teachings.

He thinks about those
teachings day and night.

—PSALM 1:1–2

Lord, tell me your ways.
Show me how to live.
Guide me in your truth.
Teach me, my God, my Savior.
I trust you all day long.
—PSALM 25:4–5

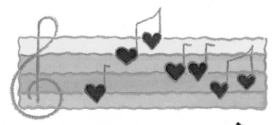

LET US LOVE HIM,
AS WE SHOULD

Lord God, you are my hope.

I have trusted you since I was young.

I have depended on you since I was born.

You have been my help from the day I was born.

I will always praise you.

—PSALM 71:5–6

I love the Lord because he listens to my prayers for help.

He paid attention to me.

So I will call to him for help as long as I live.

—PSALM 116:1–2

God, you are my God.
I want to follow you.
My whole being
thirsts for you,
like a man in a dry, empty land
where there is no water.
I have seen you in the Temple.
I have seen your strength and
glory.
Your love is better than life.

—PSALM 63:1–3

I remember you while I'm lying in bed.

I think about you through the night.

You are my help.

Because of your protection, I sing.

I stay close to you.

You support me with your right hand.

—PSALM 63:6–8

The Lord says, "If someone loves me, I will save him.

I will protect those who know me.

They will call to me, and I will answer them.

I will be with them in trouble.

I will rescue them and honor them.

I will give them a long, full life.

They will see how I can save."

—PSALM 91:14–16

You made my whole
being.

You formed me in my
mother's body.

I praise you because you
made me in an amazing and
wonderful way.

What you have done is
wonderful.

I know this very well.

—PSALM 139:13–14

I will always sing about the Lord's love.

I will tell of his loyalty from now on.

I will say, "Your love continues forever.

Your loyalty goes on and on like the sky."

—PSALM 89:1–2